A Guide for Using

the

Clifford Series

in the Classroom

Based on the book written by Norman Bridwell

This guide written by **Mary Bolte**

Illustrated by **Barb Lorseydi**

Teacher Created Materials, Inc.
6421 Industry Way
Westminister, CA 92683
www.teachercreated.com
©2000 Teacher Created Materials, Inc.
Reprinted, 2001
Made in U.S.A.
ISBN-1-57690-336-2

Table of Contents

Introduction

Clifford the dog has been a favorite canine friend of children for over 35 years. His readers and admirers have learned to recognize and cherish his unique characteristics of love, honesty, and respect. Young and old readers alike find it easy to associate themselves with the situations that Clifford encounters in each adventure.

Clifford is the beloved pet of a devoted young schoolgirl, Emily Elizabeth, who cherishes every moment with her four-legged friend. Emily watches her dog grow from the overlooked runt of the litter to a charming, kind, respected hero of the neighborhood.

Included in this popular series are a variety of books which can be used in the classroom. They involve the readers in problem-solving and thinking skills. This unit includes activities for 29 of the books, beginning with Clifford's early life as a tiny puppy and continuing with his sudden growth into "the Big Red Dog." After sharing a Clifford book with the class, refer to the Appendix (pages 43–47) for suggested activities. The generic activities on pages 18, 19, and 48 may be used with any of the selections.

A Sample Lesson Plan

The Sample Lesson Plans on page 4 provide you with a set of introductory lesson plan suggestions for three books in the series: *Clifford the Small Red Puppy, Clifford's Puppy Days,* and *Clifford the Big Red Dog,* which introduce Clifford, his early days, and his family to the reader. Each of the lessons can take from one to several days to complete and may include all or some of the suggested activities. Refer to the Suggestions for Using the Unit Activities on pages 7–10 for information relating to the unit activities.

A Unit Planner

If you wish to tailor the suggestions on pages 7–10 to a format other than the one prescribed in the Sample Lesson Plan, a blank Unit Planner is provided on page 5. Plan each day on this planner sheet by writing the activity numbers of the activities or brief notations about the lessons that you wish to accomplish. Space has been provided for reminders, comments, and other pertinent information related to each day's activities. Reproduce copies of the Unit Planner as needed.

Sample Lesson Plans

Lesson 1

1. Read Getting to Know the Books and the Author (page 6) with the students.
2. Do Before the Books activities 2, 4, 5, and 6 on page 7.
3. Read aloud *Clifford the Small Red Puppy* and *Clifford's Puppy Days.*

Lesson 2

1. Introduce the vocabulary for *Clifford the Small Red Puppy* and *Clifford's Puppy Days* on page 8.
2. Reread both stories, listening for the vocabulary words.
3. Read aloud *Clifford the Big Red Dog.*
4. Compare Clifford as a puppy to Clifford as a big dog. See Other Pocket Chart Activities on page 8.
5. Complete Petite Puppies on page 27.
6. Have the students design new dog food cans (page 38).

Lesson 3

1. Introduce the vocabulary for *Clifford the Big Red Dog* (page 8).
2. Reread the story, listening for the vocabulary words.
3. Complete the Story Questions activity on page 8, using the questions on pages 14 and 15.
4. As a whole class or individually, have the students choose one of the three books and complete The Bones of the Story on pages 18 and 19.
5. Complete How Big Is Clifford? (page 25).

Lesson 4

1. Complete The Who, What, Why, Where, and When of Clifford on page 20.
2. Help the students write more song verses in the Creative Clifford activity on page 30.
3. Compare dogs living in the city and the country, using the Venn diagram on page 37.
4. Have the students write letters to Clifford, using the stationery on page 22.

Lesson 5

1. Have the students work in small groups to plan and practice puppet shows. Use the directions and patterns on pages 16 and 17.
2. Let the students practice the Creative Clifford song(s) they wrote in Lesson 4.
3. Use the cards on page 26 to play math games. See page 9, item 3, for some activity ideas.

Lesson 6

1. Teach a lesson about verbs and follow-up with the activity sheet on page 21.
2. In pairs, the students may continue to play some of the math games with the cards from page 26.
3. Assign independent research projects on a puppy's growth to a full-grown dog. See activity 5 on page 10. Share and discuss the findings.
4. Have the students perform their puppet shows and song(s) in front of an audience.

Unit Planner

Date	Unit Activities
Date	Unit Activities
Notes/Comments:	

Date	Unit Activities
Date	Unit Activities
Notes/Comments:	

Date	Unit Activities
Date	Unit Activities
Notes/Comments:	

Getting to Know the Books and the Author

About the Books

Tiny, weak, and the runt of the litter describe Clifford as a puppy. Then a caring and inspired young city girl, Emily Elizabeth, chooses him from his brothers and sisters for her own special pet to love. Her devotion and adoration raises Clifford's self-esteem as he develops quickly into a big red dog.

The three books, *Clifford the Small Red Puppy, Clifford's Puppy Days,* and *Clifford the Big Red Dog*, trace Clifford's memorable, adventurous, and quick growth from a puppy to the "biggest red dog" on the street. Emily Elizabeth, realizing he is not perfect, overlooks his faults and looks for the best in her faithful companion. These books introduce the reader to Clifford's beginnings and prepare and motivate the reader to read other books in the series. The series conveys the message that obstacles can be overcome, and one can still be loved and forgiven.

About the Author

Norman Ray Bridwell was born in 1928 in Kokomo, Indiana. He studied art for four years and worked in commercial art for twelve years before he published his first book, *Clifford the Big Red Dog*. He enjoys making up stories that amuse children.

Norman Bridwell's real life experiences with his two children have motivated him when writing his Clifford adventures during the past 35 years. Clifford's loyal owner, Emily Elizabeth, was named after his own daughter. His son, Tim, is a character's name in other books.

Bridwell was inspired to write the first Clifford book after composing an art sample of a small girl and a big red dog. He wanted to become an illustrator, so he showed it to several editors, but it was rejected. So he wrote a story about the dog, and Scholastic Books accepted it. This was the beginning of his writing career.

Bridwell recognizes that teachers and children are very familiar with and enjoy reading the Clifford books. His stories are very effective in motivating young readers to read. Over 60 million copies of the Clifford books have been sold!

Suggestions for Using the Unit Activities

Use some or all of the following suggestions to introduce your students to Clifford in *Clifford the Small Red Puppy, Clifford's Puppy Days*, and *Clifford the Big Red Dog*, and to extend their appreciation of the books through activities that cross the curriculum. The suggested activities have been divided into three sections to assist you in planning the literature unit.

The sections are the following:

- *Before the Book:* includes suggestions for preparing the classroom environment and the students for the literature to be read
- *Into the Book:* has activities that focus on the book's content, characters, theme, etc.
- *After the Book:* extends the readers' enjoyment of the book with a culminating activity

Before the Book

1. Complete the following projects before you begin this unit:
   - Prepare the vocabulary cards (page 8) for the pocket chart.
   - Prepare the story questions (pages 14 and 15) for the pocket chart.
   - Prepare sentence strips for the pocket chart.
   - Copy and cut out the cards from page 26 for math activities.

2. Explain to the students that this unit includes 29 Clifford books, however, there are many other Clifford books and items that are not included. Display some of the books in the series. Inform the students that you will be reading and comparing the three books that introduce Clifford's beginnings, his life as a small puppy, and his growth into the "Big Red Dog."

3. Read about the author, Norman Bridwell, on page 6.

4. Set the stage for reading the books by discussing the following questions:
   - How many of you have a dog?
   - Did you get him or her as a puppy?
   - What are some of the memorable moments you have had with your dog?
   - How has your dog been a good friend to you?
   - How would it be different if you had a small dog (or a large dog)?

5. Display the covers of the three books. Ask the following questions about the covers:
   - How are they alike?
   - How are they different?
   - How has Clifford changed on the three covers?
   - How do you think this happened?
   - What would you do if your dog grew to be this big?

6. Introduce the characters in the books: Emily Elizabeth and her parents, Clifford and his family, Emily Elizabeth's Aunt Martha, and the Baker.

Suggestions for Using the Unit Activities *(cont.)*

Into the Books

1. Pocket Chart Activities

- Vocabulary Cards
  After reading the books, discuss the meanings of the following words in context. Make copies of the dog food can on page 13. Write the words on the cans. Display the cans in a pocket chart. See pages 11 and 12 for more information.

Clifford the Small Puppy

police	love	runt	landlord
city	neighbors	apartment	
upstairs	country	uncle	

Clifford's Puppy Days

wedding cake	clock	aunt	cream puffs
fetch	merry-go-round	first prize	
bake shop	whipped cream	bath	

Clifford the Big Red Dog

perfect	dog show	mistakes	first prize
games	hide-and-seek	watchdog	
problem	biggest	bad habits	

- Story Questions
  Develop critical thinking skills, using the story questions on pages 14 and 15. The questions are based on Bloom's Taxonomy and are provided for each level of Bloom's Levels of Learning. Reproduce copies of the dog bone pattern on page 13, using a different color for each of the three books. Write a question on each bone.

- Other Pocket Chart Activities
  –Brainstorm a list of sentences retelling important parts of the books. Display them in the pocket chart.
  –Write descriptions about Clifford when he was a puppy and when he was full grown. Discuss how he changed.
  –Write a list of good things about Clifford as a big dog. Then create a list of his bad habits as a big dog.

2. Language Arts

- "The Bones of the Story" (pages 18 and 19)
  Discuss the directions. Complete the story elements activity as a group or independently.

Suggestions for Using the Units Activities *(cont.)*

Into the Books *(cont.)*

- The Who, What, Why, Where, and When of Clifford (page 20)

  Allow the students to each choose one of the three books to write about. Have them each complete an outline and then write their own stories. They may share their stories with each other and/or compile them into a class book or newspaper about Clifford's adventures.

- Write a Letter (page 22)

  Ask the students to write their own letters to Clifford. They may express their reactions and feelings to his young puppy days or his adjustment to his life as a large dog.

- Action with Clifford (page 21)

  Help the students search the three Clifford books to find five verbs that describe Clifford's actions as either a puppy or a full grown dog.

- Clifford Dictionary (page 23)

  Help the students begin a class dictionary of Clifford words. When they encounter a new word in their reading ask someone to fill out a copy of page 23. Assemble these pages in a three-ring binder to be used as a classroom reference.

3. Math

- Count, Add, and Subtract With Clifford (page 26)

  Before starting this activity, copy a set of the cards onto heavy paper for each student. Discuss and follow the directions. After the cards have been completed, create addition and subtraction facts with them. For example, lay down the 4 and 5 cards and then the 9 card to show the addition fact, $4 + 5 = 9$.

  Other games might include:

    - Lay down the odd numbers or lay down the even numbers.
    - See how many ways you can add to get 10, 9, 8, etc., or see how many ways you can subtract to get 1, 2, 3, etc.
    - Create your own math games, using these cards.

- Petite Puppies (page 27)

  Discuss the directions. Provide each child with a ruler. Have them practice drawing lines which are three inches long. Then they may complete the five boxes. Discuss and compare the drawings.

- How Big is Clifford? (page 25)

  Discuss the directions and Clifford's size (as a puppy). Make comparisons between Clifford's size and items in the classroom. Review the illustrations in *Clifford the Small Red Puppy*, and find things that are bigger and smaller than Clifford.

4. Music

- Creative Clifford (page 30)

  Sing the original version of "Old Mac Donald Had a Farm." Discuss the directions, and sing the first two verses of the Clifford version. Brainstorm ideas that Clifford might think of to solve problems. This may be done together at first, and it might include a brainstorming session of rhyming words and then having the students create their own verses. When completed, compile all of the verses, and sing them for other classes or for an audience of parents.

Suggestions for Using the Units Activities *(cont.)*

Into the Books *(cont.)*

5. Science

• Clifford's Tricks (page 33)

–Discuss some of the tricks that dogs can do. Discuss the directions on the activity sheet. Have pairs of students perform the coin trick, and then compare everyone's results. Discuss whether or not the trick was always successful?

–Have the students research the normal growth pattern of a puppy from birth to adult size. Help them to measure and draw charts which show the different cycles of growth.

6. Social Studies

• Clifford in the City . . . Clifford in the Country (page 37)

–Discuss the differences between the lives of dogs who live in the city and those that live in the country. Then complete the Venn diagram as a class or assign it as individual work. The differences of living in the country belong in the top section, and the differences of living in the city belong in the bottom section. Similarities of living in both places belong in the middle section.

–Have the students research information about working dogs such as: sheep dogs, seeing-eye dogs, police dogs, Eskimo sled dogs, watchdogs, drug-sniffing dogs, etc. Compare and contrast their lives to Clifford's.

7. Art

• Design a New Dog Food Label (page 38)

–Examine a variety of dog food cans. Discuss how they could be more eye-catching. Review the directions on the activity sheet, and then brainstorm different dog food descriptive words.
–Have the students design their own cans. Display the cans on a bulletin board or have the students in other classes choose the cans that are the most eye-catching.

After the Book

Culminating Activity

• Assemble the students into small groups of four or five. Ask the groups to choose one of the three books to use as the theme for their puppet shows. Use the stick puppets on page 17 for the main characters. If extra puppets are needed for other characters, the students may create their own. Each group can have a narrator who narrates the story as the puppeteers silently act out the story, or each puppeteer may have a speaking part in the performance. Have the groups practice their presentations and when they are ready to perform, invite others to attend. (The Creative Clifford song from page 30 can also be presented at this time.)

To create the puppet theaters, refer to the directions on page 16. To create larger puppet theaters, use boxes from large appliances such as stoves, refrigerators, or televisions.

10

Pocket Chart Activities

Prepare a pocket chart for storing and using vocabulary cards, story questions, and sentence strips.

How to Make a Pocket Chart

If a commercial pocket chart is unavailable, you can make a pocket chart if you have access to a laminator. Begin by laminating a 24" x 36" (60 cm x 90 cm) piece of colored tagboard. Run about 20" (50 cm) of additional plastic. To make nine pockets, cut the clear plastic into nine equal strips. Space the strips equally down the 36" (90 cm) length of the tagboard. Attach each strip with cellophane tape along the sides and bottom. This will hold the sentence strips, word cards, etc., and can be displayed in a learning center or mounted on a chalk tray for use with a group. When your pocket chart is ready, use it to display sentence strips, vocabulary words, and question cards. A sample chart is provided below.

How to Use a Pocket Chart

1. Using three different colors, one for each Clifford book, reproduce the dog food can pattern on page 13. Make vocabulary cards as directed on page 8. Print the definitions on sentence strips for a matching activity.

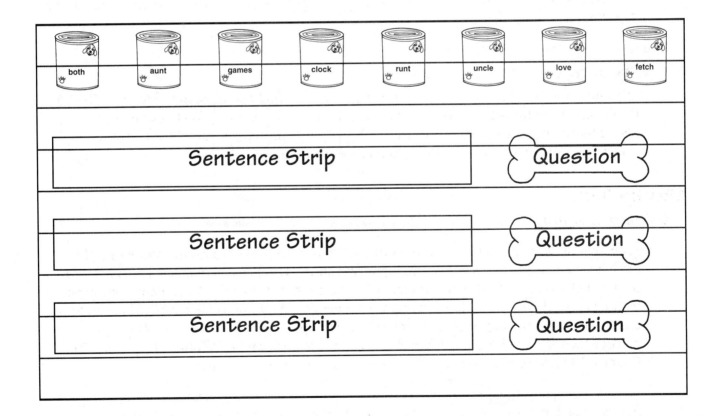

Pocket Chart Activities *(cont.)*

How to Use a Pocket Chart (cont.)

---

2. Print the titles of the three Clifford books on sentence strips. Mix up the vocabulary cards and have the students match them to each of the three stories.

3. Print the major events from each of the stories on sentence strips. Have the students place them in sequential order.

4. Reproduce the bone pattern on page 13. Use a different color for each book. For your own reference you may wish to write the appropriate Bloom's Level of Learning (Knowledge, Comprehension, Application, Analysis, Synthesis, or Evaluation) on the back. Write a story question from pages 14 and 15 on the front middle section.

5. Use the bone cards after reading each story. These will provide opportunities for the students to develop and practice higher-level critical thinking skills.

6. Arrange the students in pairs. Read the questions out loud and ask the partners to take turns answering them to each other.

7. Divide the class into two teams to play this simple game. Mix up the question cards for the three books. Ask the team members first to answer the question and then name the book to which it relates. The teams will score one point for each appropriate answer.

8. Have the students practice their oral reading skills by reading the sentence strips out loud.

Pocket Chart Patterns

See pages 11 and 12 for directions.

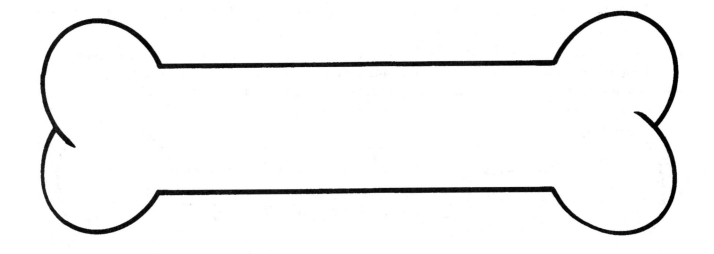

Story Questions

The following questions are based on Bloom's Levels of Learning. Prepare the dog bones (page 13) as directed on page 12. Write a different question from the Levels of Learning on each of the bones. Use the dog bones with the suggested activities.

?	**I. KNOWLEDGE** (ability to recall learned information)	**II. COMPREHENSION** (ability to master understanding of information)	**III. APPLICATION** (ability to do something new with information)
Clifford the Small Red Puppy	• Who is Emily Elizabeth? • Where does she live? • Why is Clifford put in the garden instead of the apartment? • Why do they send Clifford to the country?	• Why does Emily Elizabeth have to be careful when she plays with Clifford? • How does she get him to fall asleep? • When Clifford is lost, how does Emily Elizabeth's aunt find him? • How do they get Clifford cleaned up?	• What kind of fun do Emily Elizabeth and Clifford have together? • What are Clifford's bad habits? • Why is it difficult to keep Clifford? • What good things does Clifford do?
Clifford's Puppy Days	• Why does Emily Elizabeth choose Clifford instead of the other puppies in the litter? • Why does Clifford have a hard time acting like a regular puppy? • Why does Emily Elizabeth tell Clifford she loves him? • Why does Emily Elizabeth let Clifford sleep on her pillow?	• Why does Clifford have a hard time playing with Emily Elizabeth's toys? • Where does Clifford get lost in the apartment? • Why does Clifford have a difficult time at the bakery?	• What are the good and bad things about Clifford's large size? • Why is it difficult for Clifford to win a prize at the dog show? • Why does Emily Elizabeth decide to keep Clifford instead of the other dogs?
Clifford the Big Red Dog	• What do you think would have happened to Clifford if Emily Elizabeth had not taken him? • How would you have fed Clifford? • What would you have done with Clifford when he grew so large?	• How would you have played with Clifford when he was little? • Where would you have Clifford sleep? • How would you keep Clifford clean?	• What games would you play with Clifford? • What would you do to stop Clifford's bad habits? • Why would you like or not like to have Clifford as a pet?

Story Questions *(cont.)*

	IV. ANALYSIS (ability to examine the parts of a whole)	V. SYNTHESIS (ability to bring together information to make something new)	VI. EVALUATION (ability to form and defend an opinion)
Clifford the Small Red Puppy	• When Emily Elizabeth says that the "runt" needs her, what does she mean? • Why do you think Clifford grows with Emily Elizabeth's love? • Why do you think Clifford likes Emily Elizabeth's bed? • Why does Clifford stop growing?	• How does Emily Elizabeth help Clifford feel loved? • How does Clifford's small size cause problems? • Why do you think Emily Elizabeth's aunt and the small boy help Clifford?	• Why do you think Emily Elizabeth likes to play with Clifford? • Why do you think or not think that Clifford is a valuable dog? • How do you think Emily Elizabeth consoled Clifford after he got second prize?
Clifford's Puppy Days	• What might Emily Elizabeth have done if Clifford had remained small? • What might have happened if Clifford had stayed in the city? • What might Martha have told Emily Elizabeth about how she got her dog at a fancy pet store?	• What games would you play with the big-sized Clifford? • What kinds of toys would you have used to play with Clifford, the puppy? • How would you keep track of a small puppy like Clifford?	• What other bad habits might Big Clifford have? • What might have happened if Clifford had won first prize at the dog show?
Clifford the Big Red Dog	• Do you think large or small animals make better pets? Why or why not? • Do you think it's better to raise a dog in the city or in the country? Why or why not?	• Would you rather have a small dog or a large dog? Why or why not? • What would you have done if you were Emily Elizabeth's aunt in the bakery?	• Do you think Clifford should have won first prize in the dog show? Why or why not? • Would you keep the full-grown Clifford instead of getting another dog? Why or why not?

Stick Puppet Theaters

Make a class set of puppet theaters (one for each student) or make one theater for every two to four students. The patterns and directions for making the stick puppets are on page 17.

Materials:

- 22" x 28" (56 cm x 71 cm) pieces of colored poster board (enough for each student or group of students)
- markers, crayons, or paints
- scissors or a craft knife

Directions: Fold the poster board 8" (20 cm) in from each of the shorter sides. (See the picture below.) Cut a "window" in the front panel, large enough to accommodate two or three stick puppets. Let the children personalize and decorate their own theaters. Laminate the stick puppet theaters to make them more durable. You may wish to send the theaters home at the end of the year or save them to use year after year.

Consider the following suggestions for using the puppets and the puppet theaters:

- Prepare the stick puppets, using the directions on page 17. Use the puppets and the puppet theaters with the Readers Theater Script on pages 40 and 41. (Let small groups of students take turns reading the parts and using the stick puppets.)
- Use the stick puppets and theaters for the puppet show in the Culminating Activity described on page 10.
- Let the students experiment with the puppets by retelling Clifford books in their own words.
- Have the students create new Clifford adventures using the puppets and puppet theaters.
- If other characters are needed, have the students make their own puppets.

Stick Puppet Patterns

Directions: Reproduce the patterns on tagboard or construction paper. Have the students color the patterns and cut them out along the dashed lines. To complete the stick puppets, glue each pattern to a tongue depressor or a craft stick. Use the stick puppets with the puppet theaters, the Readers Theater Script (pages 40 and 41) and/or the Culminating Activity (page 10).

The Bones of the Story

Directions: Read a Clifford book. Write the title of the book in the first dog bone and the five story elements of the book (setting, characters, problem, events, and resolution) in the other bones. Cut out the six bones and glue them on a larger sheet of colored paper. Share your "bones of the story" with a friend.

The Bones of the Story *(cont.)*

See page 18 for directions.

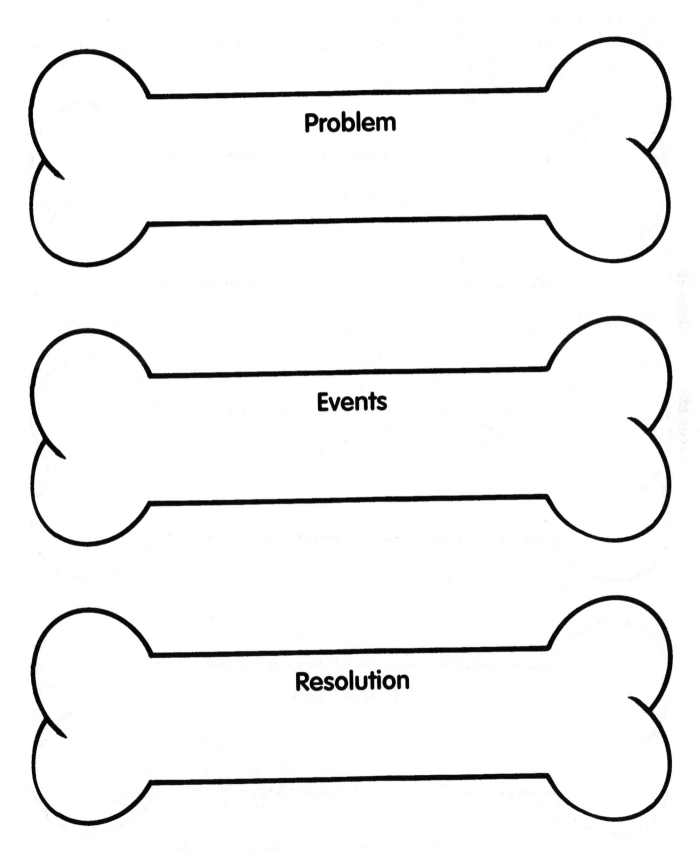

Problem

Events

Resolution

The Who, What, Why, Where, and When of Clifford

Directions: Read one of the Clifford books. Pretend that you are a reporter gathering the basic facts about the story. Write the facts on this activity sheet and then use them to write your article on a separate piece of paper. Be sure to include a title for your article.

1. **Who** were the characters? _____

   _____

   _____

2. **What** happened? _____

   _____

   _____

3. **Why** did it happened? _____

   _____

   _____

4. **Where** did it happen? _____

   _____

   _____

5. **When** did it happen? _____

   _____

   _____

Action With Clifford

Directions: Clifford is always full of action. An action word is called a verb.
Read a Clifford book and find five verbs. Write the verbs and their meanings on
the lines below. Then, in the right column, draw a picture to show each action.

1. _____

_____

_____

_____

2. _____

_____

_____

_____

3. _____

_____

_____

_____

4. _____

_____

_____

_____

5. _____

_____

_____

_____

Write a Letter

Directions: Write a letter to Clifford. Tell him what you felt about him as a puppy or ask him about his adjustment to his life as a large dog.

_____
(Date)

Dear Clifford,

_____

_____

_____

_____

_____

_____

_____

Sincerely,

_____
(Your Name)

Clifford Dictionary

Directions: Whenever you encounter a new word in your reading, fill out a copy of this page. Place the first letter of the word in the circle. For example: A is for aunt. Then draw a picture in the space to represent the word.

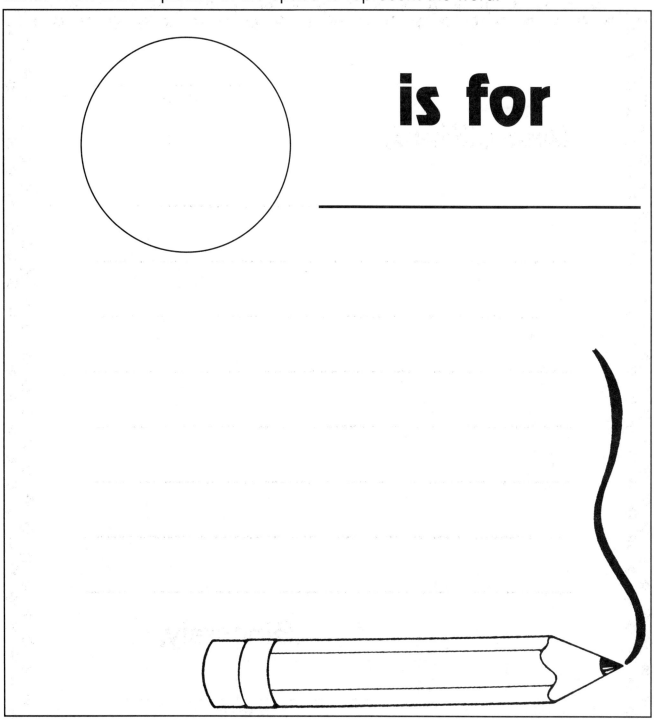

is for

_____

Teacher Directions: Collect these activity sheets and alphabetically assemble them in a three-ring binder to make a class dictionary. See the Appendix for other uses for this page.

Clifford and His Pals Search a Construction Site

Teacher Note: This activity is part of the lesson for *Clifford's Pals*. See page 45 of the appendix.

Directions: Clifford and his pals went to a construction site. Circle the 12 listed construction words in the puzzle. The words may go up, down, across, or diagonally.

Word List

crane	pit	scaffold	pipes	crew	cement
bulldozer	backhoe	cement truck	steel ball	chute	dump truck

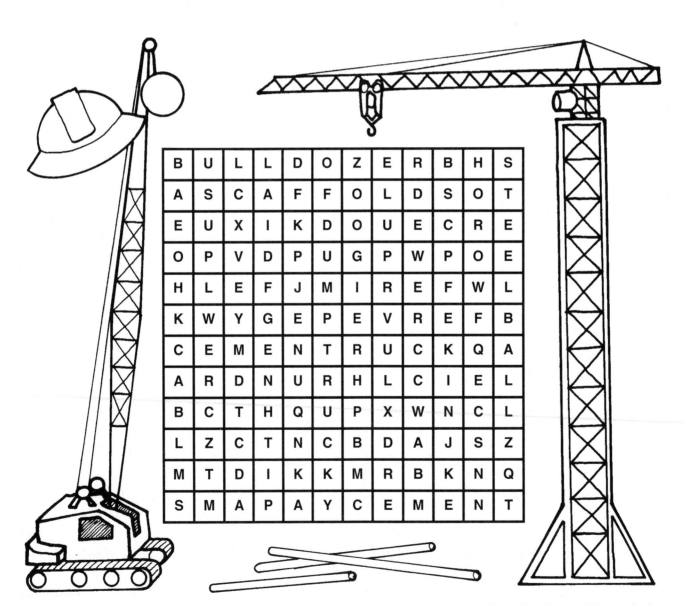

B	U	L	L	D	O	Z	E	R	B	H	S
A	S	C	A	F	F	O	L	D	S	O	T
E	U	X	I	K	D	O	U	E	C	R	E
O	P	V	D	P	U	G	P	W	P	O	E
H	L	E	F	J	M	I	R	E	F	W	L
K	W	Y	G	E	P	E	V	R	E	F	B
C	E	M	E	N	T	R	U	C	K	Q	A
A	R	D	N	U	R	H	L	C	I	E	L
B	C	T	H	Q	U	P	X	W	N	C	L
L	Z	C	T	N	C	B	D	A	J	S	Z
M	T	D	I	K	K	M	R	B	K	N	Q
S	M	A	P	A	Y	C	E	M	E	N	T

How Big Is Clifford?

Directions: After reading about Clifford as a puppy, compare his puppy size to some of the things that you saw in the illustrations. Draw pictures of what he was bigger than and what he was smaller than.

Clifford, the small red puppy . . .

is *bigger* than: is *smaller* than:

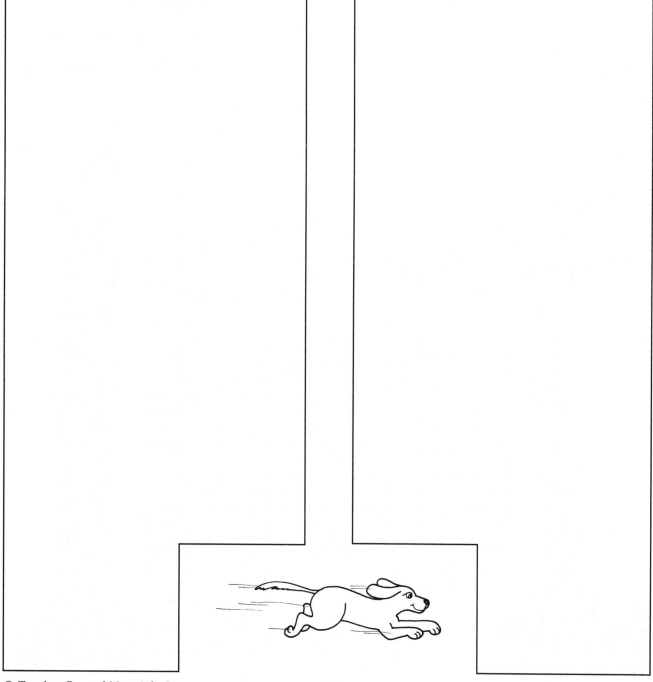

Count, Add, and Subtract With Clifford

Directions: Celebrate Clifford's birthday! Cut out the cards below. Read the words on the front of the cards. On the back of each card, write the number for the word on the front, and draw a cake with the same number of candles on it.

Teacher Note: For more activity ideas see item 3 on page 9.

Petite Puppies

Directions: When Clifford was a puppy, he was very, very small . . . smaller than a stocking cap or a large bar of soap, and he even fit into a purse. Pretend that you have a three inch long puppy. Draw your pet in the first box. Draw a food dish, a dog toy, a sleeping bed, and a doggie bathtub for your tiny puppy in the other boxes.

1. My Puppy

2. Food Dish

3. Sleeping Bed

4. Doggie Bathtub

5. Dog Toy

Clifford's Pals: Large and Small

Directions: Clifford has five dog pals: Basker, Flip, Lenny, Nero, and Susie.
Color the dogs and then cut them out. Number them in order from the smallest
to the largest, with 1 being the smallest and 5 being the largest. Glue them in
order (from the largest to the smallest) on a large piece of construction paper.
Draw Clifford and some scenery on the construction paper. Also, show where
they are going.

Susie

Lenny

Nero

Basker

Flip

One Dozen Eggs for Clifford

Teacher Note: This activity is part of the lesson for *Clifford's Happy Easter*. See page 47 of the appendix.

Directions: Clifford has a dozen Easter eggs, but they need colors and designs. Solve the problems and look for the answers below to learn how to color the eggs.

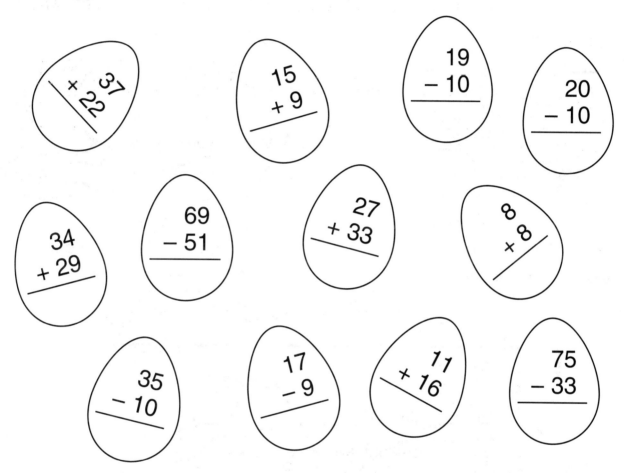

1. Color the egg with the difference of 10, blue.
2. Color the egg with the sum of 24 with yellow zigzags.
3. Color the egg with the difference of 9 with red hearts.
4. Color the egg with the sum of 59, orange.
5. Color the egg with the difference of 25 with green triangles.
6. Color the egg with the sum of 60, red.
7. Color the egg with the difference of 18, purple.
8. Color the egg with the sum of 63 with orange stripes.
9. Color the egg with the difference of 42, yellow.
10. Color the egg with the sum of 16, green.
11. Color the egg with the difference of 8 with blue squares.
12. Color the egg with the sum of 27, pink.

Creative Clifford

Directions: Be creative and finish the following song about Clifford (to the tune of "Old Mac Donald Had a Farm"). Write a third verse that tells about Clifford's problem solving ideas and then sing the song.

Verse 1

Clifford, Clifford is my name.
Ye-ow, woof-woof, ye-ow.
I'm on my way to the Hall of Fame.
Ye-ow, woof-woof, ye-ow.
With a ye-ow yow here,
And a ye-ow yow there,
Here a woof, there a woof.
Everywhere a woof-woof.
Clifford, Clifford is my name.
Ye-ow, woof-woof, ye-ow.

Verse 2

Clifford, Clifford is really great.
Ye-ow, woof-woof, ye-ow.
Super ideas he can create.
Ye-ow, woof-woof, ye-ow.
With a ye-ow yow here,
And a ye-ow yow there,
Here a woof, there a woof.
Everywhere a woof-woof.
Clifford, Clifford is really great.
Ye-ow, woof-woof, ye-ow.

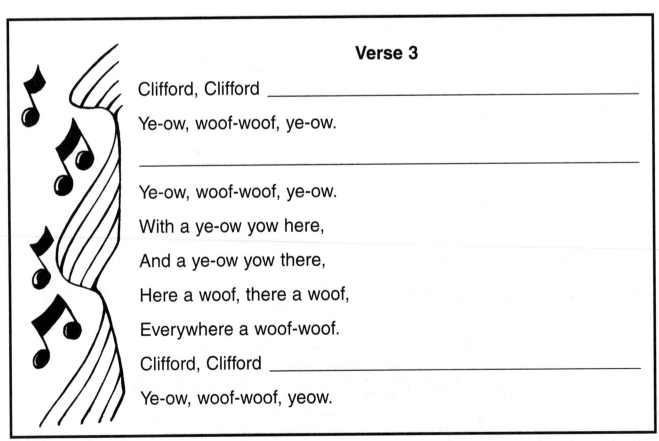

Verse 3

Clifford, Clifford _____

Ye-ow, woof-woof, ye-ow.

_____

Ye-ow, woof-woof, ye-ow.

With a ye-ow yow here,

And a ye-ow yow there,

Here a woof, there a woof,

Everywhere a woof-woof.

Clifford, Clifford _____

Ye-ow, woof-woof, yeow.

What Happened to the Shell?

Teacher Note: This activity is part of the lesson for *Clifford's Happy Easter.* See page 47 of the appendix.

Directions: In *Clifford's Happy Easter*, Clifford tried hard to not break the shells of the eggs, but his paws were just too big. A less messy way of removing a shell from an egg is by placing it in vinegar. Place a hard boiled egg in a jar of vinegar. Screw the lid on the jar. Periodically observe the egg for three days. Complete the activity below as you observe the changes in the egg.

Egg Observations

1. Look and feel the egg before you put it in the vinegar. List six words that describe it.

_____   _____   _____

_____   _____   _____

2. What did the egg look like after you took it out of the vinegar?

_____

3. How did the egg feel after you took it out of the vinegar?

_____

4. What do you see through the membrane of the egg?

_____

5. Why did the shell disappear?

_____

6. Why is an egg's shell important to the living creature inside of it?

_____

Every Day Is Earth Day

Teacher Note: This activity is part of the lesson for *Clifford's Spring Clean-up.* See page 47 of the appendix.

Directions: Earth Day is usually held in April, and it is a day when people do something special to clean their neighborhoods and preserve our planet. In *Clifford's Spring Clean-up*, Clifford helps his neighbors clean up a vacant lot. Now, it's your turn. Plan a clean-up project for your home, school, or neighborhood. Take before and after photographs or draw your own pictures in the boxes below. Share your project results with your classmates.

Before

After

Clifford's Tricks!

Teacher Note: This activity is part of the lesson for *Clifford's Tricks*. See page 43 of the appendix.

Directions: Clifford likes to do tricks. You can perform tricks too. With a partner, read and follow the coin trick directions below. You will need three coins and a blindfold. Only one partner should read the directions at a time. This person will be called Player #1 in the directions. The other person will be Player #2.

— The Magic Coin —

1. Player #1 lays out three coins on the desk and is then blindfolded.

2. Player #2 picks up one of the coins, holds it, and counts to 15.

3. Next, player #2 puts the coin back on the desk.

4. Player #1 touches each of the coins and picks up the one that is the warmest. It should be the same coin that Player #2 held.

5. Player #2 is given the opportunity to guess how the correct coin was chosen.

After the secret is revealed (the warmest coin is the "magic coin" because it was just held), both players should have the chance to try the trick over and over. Is the trick always successful? Why or Why not?

Clifford Takes a Trip

Teacher Note: This activity is part of the lesson for *Clifford Takes a Trip.* See page 43 of the appendix.

Directions: Find the number 1 at the top of Clifford's Map (page 35). Tell what happens to Clifford as he tries to find Emily Elizabeth and her family. Write your answers on the lines below.

1. _____
_____

2. _____
_____

3. _____
_____

4. _____
_____

5. _____
_____

6. _____
_____

7. _____
_____

8. _____
_____

9. _____
_____

10. _____
_____

Clifford Takes a Trip *(cont.)*

Now It's Your Turn!

Teacher Note: This activity is part of the lesson for *Clifford Goes to Hollywood.* See page 44 of the appendix.

Directions: In *Clifford Goes to Hollywood*, Clifford has to take a screen test to show that he is a good actor. Now it's your turn!

Find a partner. One person will have the job of the movie director and the other will be the actor. The actor will act out the feelings listed below, while the movie director will judge his or her performances. The actor will receive three stars (☆☆☆) for an excellent job, two stars (☆☆) for a good job, and a single star (☆) if the performance needs more practice.

When you are finished, switch roles. Discuss your screen tests with each other.

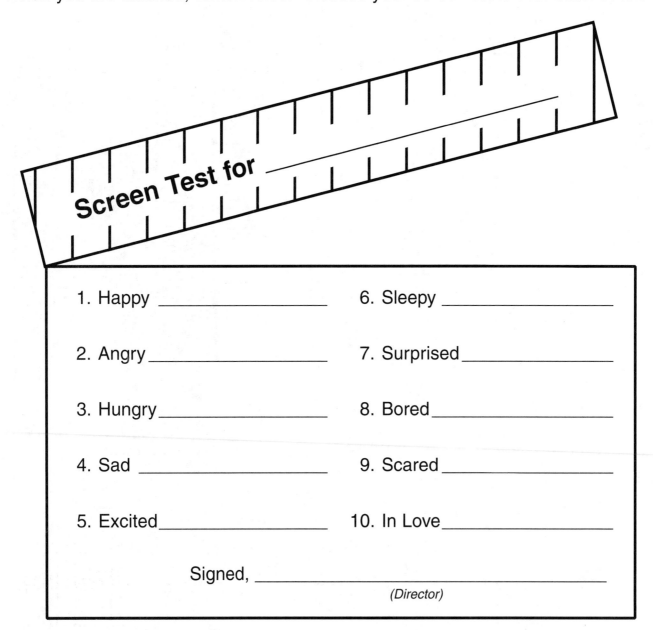

Screen Test for _____

1. Happy _____	6. Sleepy _____
2. Angry _____	7. Surprised _____
3. Hungry _____	8. Bored _____
4. Sad _____	9. Scared _____
5. Excited _____	10. In Love _____

Signed, _____
(Director)

Clifford in the City . . . Clifford in the Country

Teacher Note: This activity is part of the lesson for *Clifford's Family*. See page 44 of the appendix.

Directions: Clifford's mother, sister (Claudia), and brother (Nero) live in the city. His sister Bonnie lives in the country. Write the differences between living in the country and living in the city in the outer parts of the Venn diagram. Write the ways that living in the city and the country are alike in the middle section of the Venn diagram.

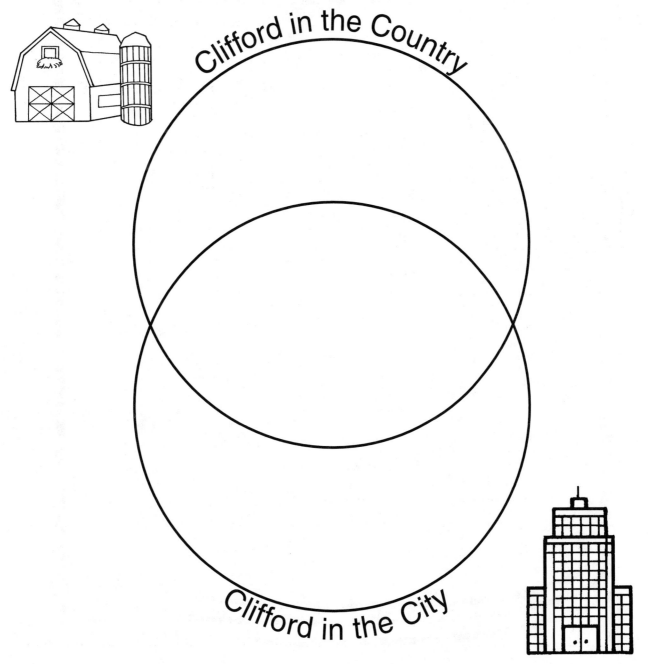

Design a New Dog Food Label

Directions: Clifford loves dog food, but his dog food comes in plain, blue cans. Design a new dog food can with a label that will attract buyers. Be sure to include its name, using descriptive words. Share your can with a friend.

Clifford's Colorful Emotions

Directions: Clifford was feeling blue, which means he was feeling sad and unhappy. Sad and unhappy are adjectives. An adjective is a word that describes a noun. Color the six listed colors on the color wheel and then write adjectives to tell how each color makes you feel.

(**Reminder:** The primary colors are red, yellow, and blue. They are the colors from which the other colors are made. The secondary colors are purple, orange, and green. Each of these are created by mixing two primary colors.)

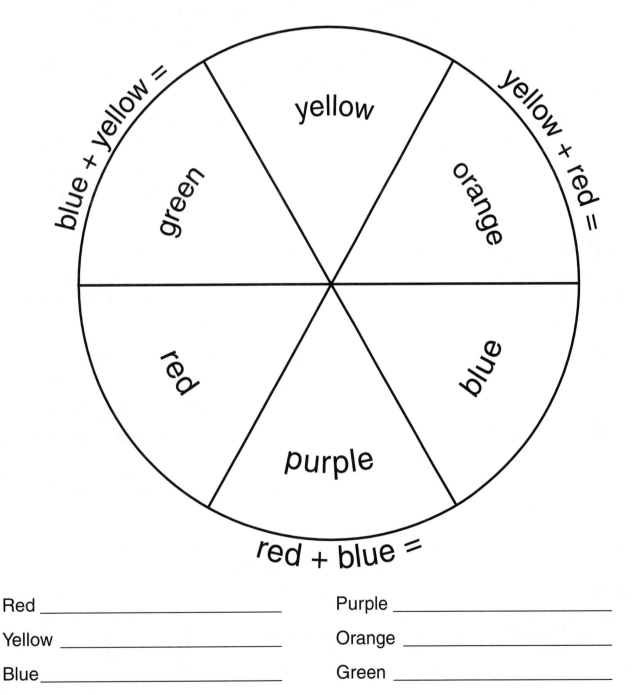

Red _____   Purple _____

Yellow _____   Orange _____

Blue _____   Green _____

Readers Theater Script

Characters

Emily Elizabeth   Clifford 3
Clifford 1   Clifford 4
Clifford 2   Clifford 5

Emily Elizabeth: Hi! My name is Emily Elizabeth, and I have a big, red dog named Clifford. I taught him good manners, and everyone loves him, because he is so kind.

Clifford 1: When I want something, I always say "please."

Clifford 2: When someone gives me something, I always say "thank you" or send a thank you note.

Clifford 3: I love to go to the movies, and I always wait for my turn when I'm in line to buy a ticket.

Clifford 4: I love to eat snacks at the movies, and I always put the empty bags and containers into the litter baskets to keep the theater clean.

Clifford 5: When I pass in front of people to find my seat, I say "Excuse me."

Clifford 1: I am quiet during the movie so that everyone else can hear and enjoy the show.

Clifford 2: I hold a tissue or a handkerchief over my nose and mouth when I sneeze.

Clifford 3: My friends like to play with me, and I share my toys with them.

Clifford 4: When we are finished playing with the toys, we put them away instead of leaving them all over the place.

Clifford 5: I am really good at playing tennis, and I always play by the rules.

Clifford 1: Sometimes I disagree with the other tennis player, so we talk it over before we start playing again.

Clifford 2: Being a good sport makes the game fun. I smile even when I lose, and I am happy when I win. I always congratulate the losers and tell them they played a good game.

Readers Theater Script *(cont.)*

Clifford 3:   It's fun to visit my sister in the country. I always call ahead to let her know that I'm coming.

Clifford 4:   I arrive on time and knock on the door before I walk in. I also wipe my dirty feet before I go in.

Clifford 5:   Then I kiss my sister and shake paws with her friends.

Clifford 1:   Before we eat dinner, I wash my paws so that they are clean before I touch my food.

Clifford 2:   I chew my food with my mouth shut and I don't talk until after I have swallowed my food.

Clifford 3:   I help everyone clean up and put things away.

Clifford 4:   Then I say "thank you" and "good-bye" to my sister and her friends.

Clifford 5:   Everybody loves my good manners and that's why everybody loves me!

Emily Elizabeth: Remember all of Clifford's good manners and behave like he does and you will have lots of friends too!

Variations for Performance

- Make masks for the characters.

- Make decorative bone-shaped name tags to identify the characters.

 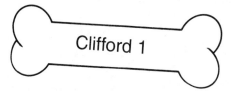

- There can be two casts. One can read the script while the other pantomimes the actions of the characters.

- All performers can stand with their backs to the audience. When a performer reads his or her lines, he or she turns, faces the audience, and reads. When finished, the performer turns his or her back to the audience again.

- At the end of the reading, have the audience repeat and act out Clifford's manners.

Bibliography

Below is a list of Clifford books used in this literature unit. They were all written by Norman Bridwell and published by Scholastic Inc. (555 Broadway, New York, NY 10012). **Note:** Titles with asterisks are also available in Spanish.

Clifford the Big Red Dog	1963		*Count on Clifford*	1985
Clifford Gets a Job	1965		*Clifford's Pals*	1985
Clifford Takes a Trip	1966		*Clifford's Manners*	1987
Clifford's Halloween	1966		*Clifford's Birthday Party*	1988
Clifford's Tricks	1969		*Clifford's Puppy Days*	1989
Clifford the Small Red Puppy	1972		*Clifford's Word Book*	1990
Clifford's Riddles	1974		*Clifford, We Love You*	1991
Clifford's Good Deeds	1975		*Clifford's Thanksgiving Visit*	1993
Clifford at the Circus	1977		*Clifford the Firehouse Dog*	1994
Clifford Goes to Hollywood	1980		*Clifford's Happy Easter*	1994
Clifford's ABC	1983		*Clifford and the Big Storm*	1995
Clifford's Kitten	1984		*Clifford's Sports Day*	1996
Clifford's Family	1984		*Clifford's Spring Clean-up*	1997
Clifford's Christmas	1984		*Clifford's First Autumn*	1997
Clifford and the Grouchy Neighbors	1985			

Appendix

Activities for Other Clifford Books

The following is a list of suggested activities for 26 other Clifford books. The students may use the generic activity sheet on page 48 for any or all of the listed titles. Collect these and put them in a place that all of the students will be able to refer to them.

Clifford Gets a Job

1. Research jobs that dogs perform (for example: police dogs, seeing-eye dogs, sled dogs, etc.).
2. Experiment with actions and uses of hula hoops.
3. Examine the words and numbers on different kinds of dog food cans and boxes. Discuss them.
4. Discuss why rats are bad for a farm.
5. Invite a member of the K-9 division of your local police department to talk to the class.

Clifford Takes a Trip

1. Complete Clifford Takes a Trip on pages 34 and 35.
2. Research how bears care for and protect their young.
3. Write a story about a memorable trip you took.
4. Create a picture postcard about a place you would like to visit.

Clifford's Halloween

1. Create and draw a new Halloween costume for Clifford.
2. Brainstorm a list of things that you can do with an apple. Choose one of these things and do it.
3. Share favorite apple recipes and prepare one in class.
4. Write a scary story and share it with a friend. Did your friend really think it was scary?

Clifford's Tricks

1. Complete Clifford's Tricks on page 33.
2. Have a debate. Compare and determine who was the better dog, Bruno or Clifford.
3. Perform a trick for the class.
4. Invite a dog trainer or owner to discuss how dogs are taught to obey commands.

Clifford's Riddles

1. Write some riddles. Compile all of the class' riddles into a book.
2. Read and share riddle books.
3. Brainstorm a list of rhyming pairs and then create riddles relating to the pairs.
4. Choose your favorite Clifford riddle and illustrate it.
5. Create math word problems, using up to 50 cans of dog food. (For example: Clifford had 50 cans of dog food. He ate 45 cans of dog food. How many are left?)

Clifford's Good Deeds

1. Present everyday problems, and discuss how you could perform good deeds to help solve them.
2. Write a paragraph about how you performed a good deed.
3. Brainstorm a list of fire safety rules and then create posters which display these safety rules.
4. Invite a firefighter to visit the class and tell about his or her career.
5. Design a new hero medal for Clifford.

Appendix *(cont.)*

Clifford at the Circus

1. Complete The Bones of the Story (pages 18 and 19) about this book.
2. Write the words that you see on the signs in the book. Put them in alphabetical order.
3. Draw an elephant parade of five elephants. Put them in order by size, the leader being the largest.
4. Make up math word problems about throwing pies at Clifford. (for example: I had 12 pies. I threw five at Clifford. How many are left?)

Clifford Goes to Hollywood

1. Complete Now It's Your Turn! on page 36.
2. Write about why you would or would not like to be a movie star.
3. Research Hollywood, California, to find out more about the city.
4. Watch a movie as a class and then discuss what you think of the movie.

Clifford's ABC

1. Create class or individual ABC books, using themes such as animals, toys, names, food, fruits, or vegetables. Make 26 copies (one for each letter of the alphabet) of The Clifford Dictionary on page 23. Design a cover and compile the pages into a book.
2. Learn how to alphabetize words to the second and third letters. Alphabetize lists of words.
3. Create a class ABC list of words including items in the classroom.

Clifford's Kitten

1. Experiment with weighing heavy and light objects, and then find objects of equal weight.
2. Compare the differences and similarities between cats and dogs, including physical characteristics, habits, and daily lifestyles.
3. Complete The Who, What, Why, Where, and When of Clifford on page 20.
4. Write a paragraph explaining why you would rather be a cat or a dog.
5. Visit the local animal shelter or ask a representative to speak to the class about homeless animals.

Clifford's Family

1. Complete Clifford in the City . . . Clifford in the Country on page 37.
2. Create a poster of your family.
3. Bulls do not like red. How many red things can you draw?
4. Prepare a short speech about your family. Have a class Family Day where you can share your speech with the class. Families may be invited to attend.

Clifford's Christmas

1. Discuss Christmas and other holiday traditions that are symbolic in your family (or in a family that you know). Invite family members to share them with the class.
2. Use snow, clay, or foam to create animals, cars, toys, etc.
3. Research the different kinds of evergreens that are used for Christmas trees.
4. Create a gift for Clifford. Tell why you think he will like it.

Appendix *(cont.)*

Clifford and the Grouchy Neighbors

1. Write a letter to a neighbor, and describe why you like him or her for a neighbor.
2. Complete The Bones of the Story on pages 18 and 19.
3. Sing the Creative Clifford song on page 30. Compose new verses about the events in this story.
4. Create a skit which presents the differences between good neighbors and bad neighbors.

Count on Clifford

1. Complete the Count, Add, and Subtract With Clifford activity on page 26.
2. Play math games with the Clifford cards (page 26). See the math section on page 9.
3. Make a counting book, using the Clifford Dictionary activity sheet on page 23. Instead of a letter, put a number in the circle and then put the number word on the line. Draw a picture to correspond with the number. Compile the pages to make a class book or individual books.
4. Plan a class birthday party. Make a shopping list of all the items and amounts you will need for the party. Correlate your plans with the book, *Clifford's Birthday Party*. (See below.)

Clifford's Pals

1. Complete Clifford's Pals: Large and Small on page 28.
2. Complete Clifford and His Pals Search a Construction Site on page 24.
3. Write a poem or story about one of your pals. Share it with him or her.

Clifford's Manners

1. Complete the Readers Theater activity on pages 40 and 41.
2. Write a thank you letter to someone.
3. Brainstorm words and phrases which are related to good manners like "thank you", "please", "share", and "excuse me".

Clifford's Birthday Party

1. List in order by month, the birthdays of everyone in the class and then plan a whole class birthday party. Combine this activity with the fourth activity listed under *Count on Clifford*. (See above.)
2. Compare and contrast Clifford's birthdays in this book and in *Count on Clifford*.
3. Pretend Clifford went to the beauty parlor. Create a new look for him on paper.
4. Write a story about the perfect gift.

Clifford's Word Book

1. Pick one page from this book and write its words in alphabetical order.
2. Draw a floor plan of your classroom. Include large items like the chalkboard, desks, and chairs. Label the items that you drew.
3. Write a list of the adults that you know and their careers. Interview one of them and discover more about his or her career. Use The Who, What, Why, Where, and When of Clifford activity sheet on page 20.
4. Use copies of the Clifford Dictionary activity sheet (page 23) for a book extension. Choose words from the book to put in alphabetical order. Title this new book, Clifford's ABC Word Book.

Appendix *(cont.)*

Clifford, We Love You

1. Complete Clifford's Colorful Emotions on page 39.
2. Write a paragraph about how you would cheer up a friend who might be feeling sad.
3. Sing the song, "It's Clifford!", found at the end of the book.
4. Sing Creative Clifford on page 30.

Clifford's Thanksgiving Visit

1. Write a story about a special Thanksgiving that you remember.
2. Research city transportation (cars, trucks, buses, subways, boats, airplanes, etc.).
3. Draw a picture of a city scene. Tell why you would like or dislike living in the city.
4. Compose a list of things for which you are thankful.

Clifford the Firehouse Dog

1. Make posters which show fire safety rules. See the last page of the book for ideas.
2. Research fire rescue and fire rescue dogs.
3. Visit a firehouse and learn more about the careers of firefighters.
4. Conduct stop, drop, and roll drills.
5. Look for the nearest fire hydrant to your home.
6. Complete the Action With Clifford activity on page 21.
7. Discuss what it means to be an "Honorary" of something.

Clifford's Happy Easter

1. Complete What Happened to the Shell? on page 31.
2. Complete One Dozen Eggs for Clifford on page 29.
3. Use food colors or paints to mix primary colors and form secondary colors. Refer to the color wheel in Clifford's Colorful Emotions on page 39.
4. Have an Easter egg hunt. Put each of the 15 words in the sentence below into 15 separate plastic eggs. Hide the eggs. When all of the eggs have been found put the words in order to form this sentence: Clifford and Emily Elizabeth went on an Easter egg hunt to find a lucky egg.

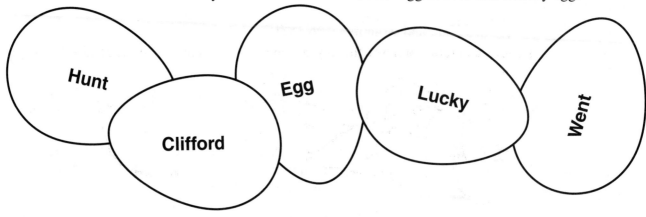

Appendix *(cont.)*

Clifford and the Big Storm

1. Explore different kinds of weather storms (for example, tornadoes, hurricanes, and blizzards).

2. Learn and practice safety rules for different kinds of storms.

3. Compare living near the ocean to living in the country.

4. Create something from sand. Write a paragraph describing how you made it.

Clifford's Sports Day

1. Have a class or school Sports Day. Include races, tugs-of-war, and other competitions.

2. Interview a physical education teacher or coach to learn more about his or her job.

3. Write a story about your favorite sport and share it with the class.

4. Discuss how numbers are used in the scores of different sports.

Clifford's Spring Clean-up

1. Tell how you would clean a room in your home.

2. Complete Everyday is Earth Day on page 32.

3. Research the recycling process and how you can contribute to its success.

4. Visit a recycling center.

Clifford's First Autumn

1. Compare the changes that you see in your part of the country during the fall season to the changes in other sections of the country.

2. Design a leaf collage. Create a math word problem using the number of leaves in the collage.

3. Research the following questions: Why do leaves change colors? Why do birds fly south for the winter?

4. Design a chart, displaying the sports played in the fall.

5. Conduct a taste test, and rank by flavor the different types of apples. Graph the results.

Book Review

Directions: After you read a Clifford book, fill in the information below. Do this for each book that you read.

Title_____

Author_____

Characters _____

_____

Setting _____

_____

The story was about_____

_____

_____

_____.

My favorite part was_____

_____

_____

_____.

I would/would not recommend this book to a friend because
(*circle one*)

_____

_____

_____